Audio Access Included - *Recorded Accompaniments Online*

# AMERICAN ART SONGS
# FOR THE PROGRESSING
## BARITONE/BASS

ISBN 978-1-4950-8856-8

To access companion recorded piano accompaniments online, visit:
www.halleonard.com/mylibrary

Enter Code
2829-8794-9945-3732

## G. SCHIRMER, Inc.

DISTRIBUTED BY
**HAL•LEONARD®**
7777 W. BLUEMOUND RD. P.O. BOX 13819 MILWAUKEE, WI 53213

www.musicsalesclassical.com
www.halleonard.com

Pianists on the recordings: [1]Brendan Fox, [2]Laura Ward

# SHENANDOAH

American Sea Chanty
Arranged by Celius Dougherty

Fare - well, my dear - est, __ I'm bound to leave you; Hi - o! you roll-ing riv - er, O Shen - an - do - ah, __ I'll not de - ceive you, Hi - o! I'm bound a - way, 'Cross the wide Mis - sou - ri.

# HEY NONNY NO!

Anonymous (16th century)

Samuel Barber

**With boisterous good-humor!**

Hey non-ny no! Hey non-ny no! Men are fools _ that wish to

die! _____

Is't not fine to dance and sing ___ When the bells of death do ring?

Is't not fine to swim in wine, ___ And turn up-on the toe, ___

*faster* _ _ _ _ _ _ _

And sing ___ hey non-ny no! When the winds blow and the seas flow?

*slower* _ _ _ *a tempo*

Hey non-ny no! ___ Hey non-ny no! Hey non-ny no!

[*cresc.*] [*f*]

*faster* _ _ _ _ _ _ _ _ *molto rit.* *a tempo*

Men are fools ___ that wish to die! ___

*8va* - - - - - - - - - - - - - - - - - - - - - - -

*To Daisy*
# THE DAISIES
from *Three Songs*

James Stephens

Samuel Barber
Op. 2, No. 1

*In Stephens' poem the word is "happily," which Barber chose to set on two notes rather than three.

# CABIN

Tennessee Williams

Paul Bowles

# SOMETIMES I FEEL LIKE A MOTHERLESS CHILD

African-American Spiritual
Arranged by Harry T. Burleigh

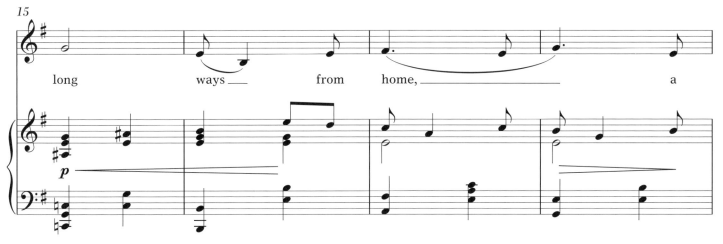

long ways __ from home, _____ a

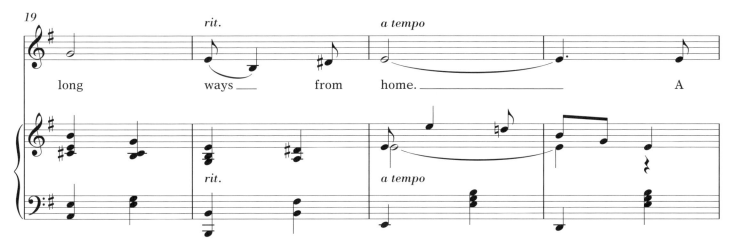

long ways __ from home. _____ A

long ways __ from home, _____ a

long ways __ from home. _____

ways ___ from home, _____ a long ways ___ from

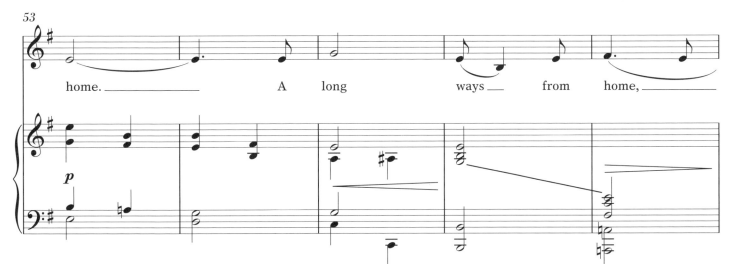

home. _____ A long ways ___ from home, _____

*rit. e dim.*                                                    *a tempo*

a long ways ___ from home. _____

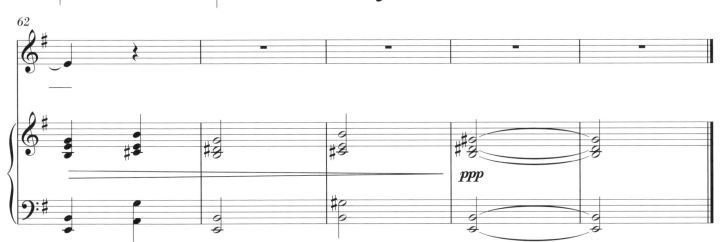

*in memory of my brother, Ralph*

# ACROSS THE WESTERN OCEAN

Irish Sea Chanty
Arranged by Celius Dougherty

say good-bye, Oh, sai - lor, where you ___ bound to?

Sis - ters, broth - ers, ___ don't you ___ cry, O'er the west - ern ___

o - cean. Oh, the

times are hard and the wa - ges ___ low, Oh, sai - lor, where you

# COLORADO TRAIL

American Folksong
Arranged by Celius Dougherty

*To Lawrence Tibbett*

# LOVELIEST OF TREES

A. E. Housman*

John Duke

* Poem from "A Shropshire Lad." Printed by permission of Grant Richards, London, publisher.

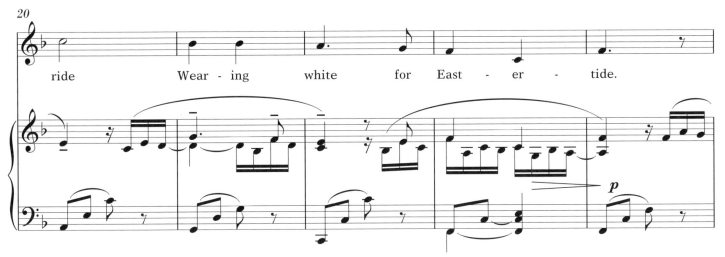

ride    Wear - ing   white   for   East - er - tide.

Now,   of   my   three - score   years   and   ten.

Twen - ty   will   not   come   a - gain,     And

take from sev-en-ty springs a score, It on - ly

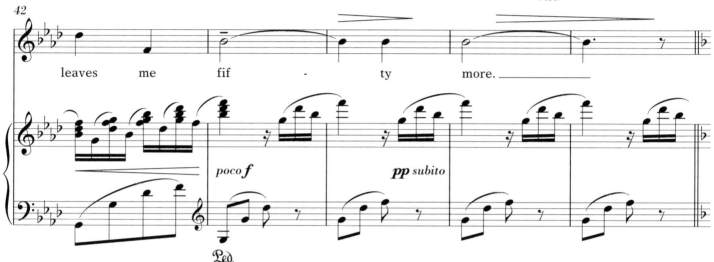

leaves me fif - ty more.

And since to look at things in bloom

Fif - ty springs are lit - tle room,

A - bout the wood - lands I will go To

see the cher - ry hung with

snow.

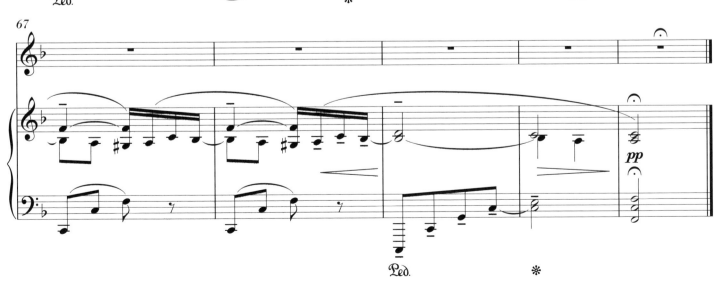

*for Olive Endres*
# THE SHEPHERD

William Blake

Lee Hoiby

all __ the day _____ And his tongue shall be

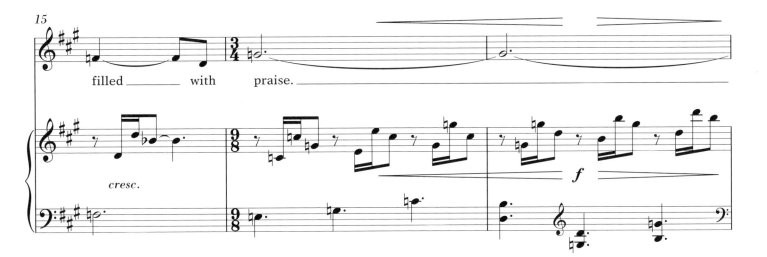

filled _____ with praise. _____

For he hears _____ the lamb's in - no - cent call. __

And __ he hears _____ the ewe's

ten - der _____ re - ply.                                    He is

watch - ful  when they are in peace,              For  they  know   when their

shep - herd  is      nigh. _____

*to the Guide*
# WHERE THE MUSIC COMES FROM

Words and Music by
Lee Hoiby

how. I want to sing to the ear-ly morn - ing, See the

sun - light melt the snow; And oh, _____ I want to

grow. _____

I want to

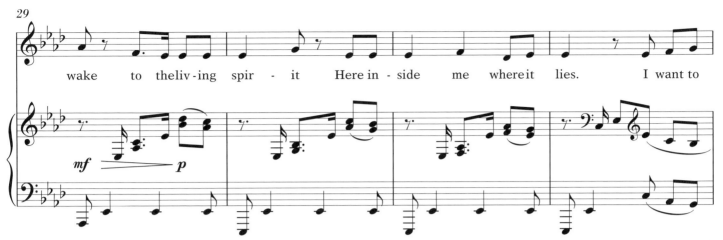

wake to the liv-ing spir - it Here in - side me where it lies. I want to

lis - ten till I can hear it, Let it guide me, and re - al - ize That I can

go with the flow un - end - ing, That is blend - ing, that is

real; And oh,_____ I want to

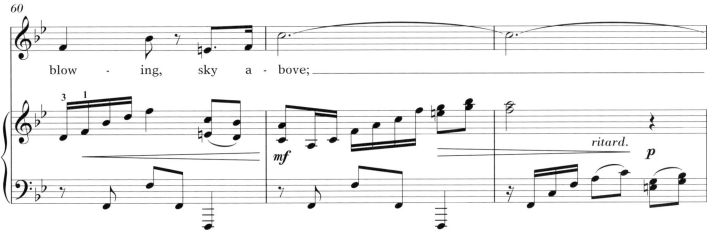

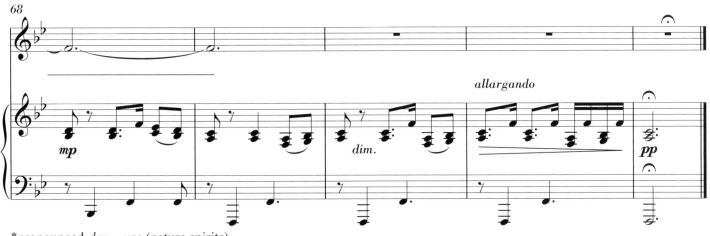

*pronounced *day – vas* (nature spirits)

# BLACK IS THE COLOR
# OF MY TRUE LOVE'S HAIR

Text collected and adapted by
John Jacob Niles
Music by John Jacob Niles

love _____ the grass where - on she stands.

I _____

love my _ love and _ well she knows, I love _____ the grass where-

on she goes; If _ she on _ earth no _ more _ I _ see, My

* Troublesome Creek, which empties into the Kentucky River.

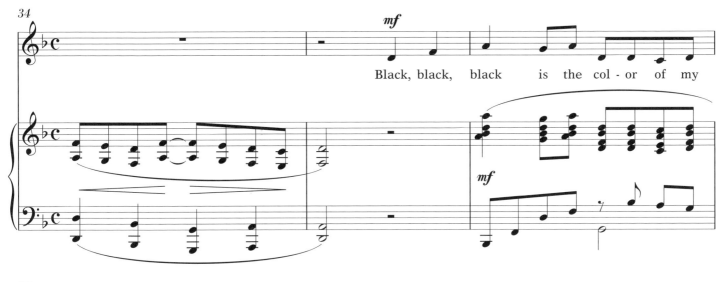

Black, black, black is the col - or of my

true love's hair, Her lips _____ are some-thing ro - sy fair, The _

pert - est _ face and the dain - ti - est _ hands– I love _____ the grass where-

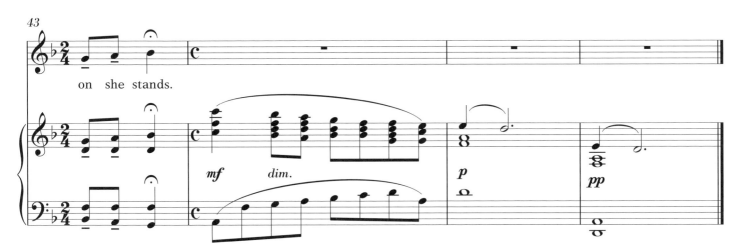

on she stands.

# BROTHER WILL, BROTHER JOHN

Elizabeth Charles Welborn

John Sacco

ain't no use, Mis - ter, af - ter you're gone, __ You

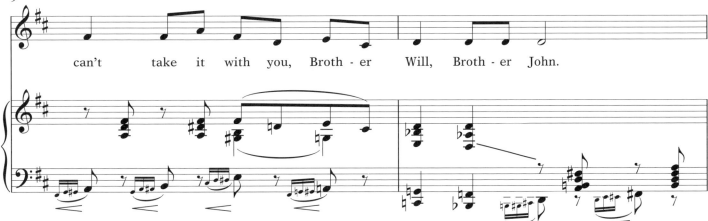

can't take it with you, Broth - er Will, Broth - er John.

You need - n't squeeze your coin tight in your hand, No

place for small change in the Prom - ised Land. It

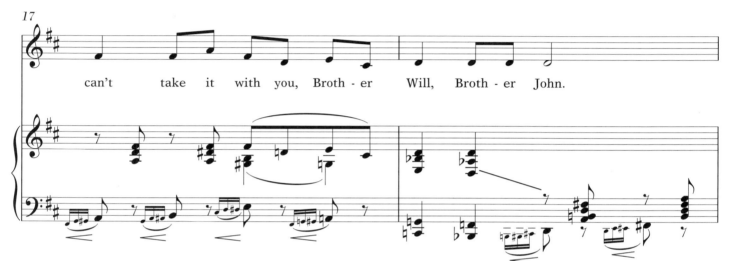

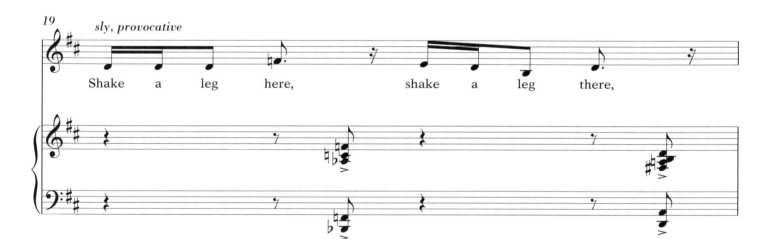

Will, Broth-er John, Broth-er Will, Broth-er John, Broth-er

Will, Broth-er John.

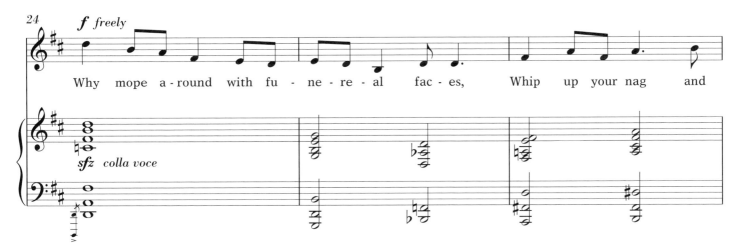

Why mope a-round with fu-ne-re-al fac-es, Whip up your nag and

loos-en the trac-es. Take a lit-tle joy, take a lit-tle plea-sure,

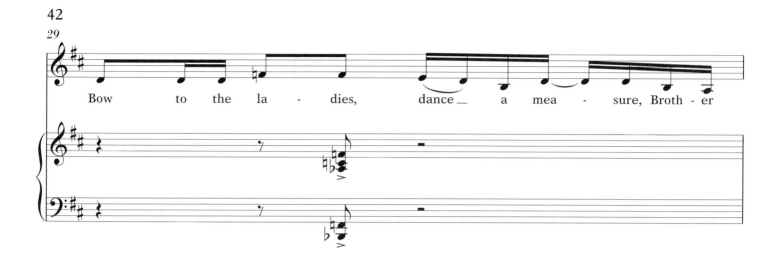

Bow to the la - dies, dance __ a mea - sure, Broth - er

Will, Broth-er John, Broth-er Will, Broth-er John, Broth-er

Will, Broth-er John.

You'll have to leave it when the cof - fin lid's on, ___ You

can't take it with you, Broth - er Will, Broth - er John, Broth - er

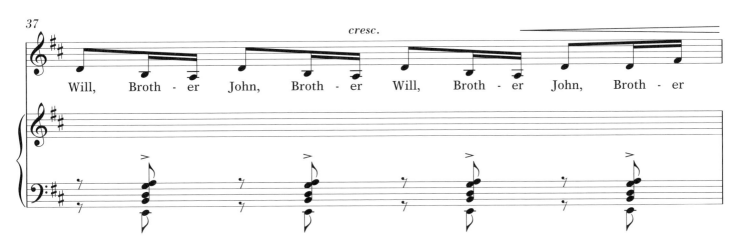

Will, Broth - er John, Broth - er Will, Broth - er John, Broth - er

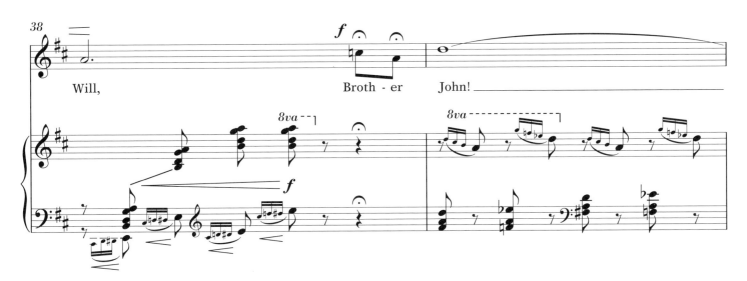

Will, Broth - er John!

# ORPHEUS WITH HIS LUTE

William Shakespeare

William Schuman

show'rs There had made a last-ing spring. _____ Ev-'ry thing that heard him

play, E-ven the bil-lows of the sea, Hung their heads, and then lay

by. _____ In sweet mu-sic is such art, Kill-ing care and grief of

heart, Fall a-sleep, or hear-ing, die. _____

# THE SEA
## from *8 Songs*

Edward MacDowell
Op. 47, No. 7

**Broadly, with rhythmic swing**

One sails a - way to sea, to sea, One stands on the shore and cries; The ship goes down the world, and the light On the sul - len wa - ter dies. On the sul - len wa - ter dies.

ship lies wrecked, Lies wrecked on the un - known deep; _____ Far

un - der, dead in his cor - al bed, The lov - er lies a-

sleep, _____ Far un - der, dead in his cor - al bed The lov - er lies a-

sleep, _____ a - sleep. _____